THE ANCIENT
CHINESE

By Jessica Cohn

Gareth Stevens
Publishing

Please visit our website, www.garethstevens.com. For a free color catalog of all our high-quality books, call toll free 1-800-542-2595 or fax 1-877-542-2596.

Library of Congress Cataloging-in-Publication Data
Cohn, Jessica.
The ancient Chinese / Jessica Cohn.
    p. cm.   (Crafts from the past)
Includes index.
ISBN 978-1-4339-7698-8 (pbk.)
ISBN 978-1-4339-7699-5 (6-pack)
ISBN 978-1-4339-7697-1 (library binding)
1. China Civilization To 221 B.C.Juvenile literature.
2. China Civilization 221 B.C.-960 A.D.Juvenile literature. I. Title.
DS741.65.C64 2013
931dc23

                              2012004814

First Edition
Published in 2013 by
Gareth Stevens Publishing
111 East 14th Street, Suite 349
New York, NY 10003

Produced by Netscribes Inc.
Art Director Dibakar Acharjee
Editorial Content The Wordbench
Copy Editor Sarah Chassé
Picture Researcher Sandeep Kumar G
Designer Ravinder Kumar
Illustrators Ashish Tanwar, Indranil Ganguly, Prithwiraj Samat and Rohit Sharma

Photo credits:
t = top, a = above, b = below, l = left, r = right, c = center
Front Cover: Netscribes Inc., Shutterstock Images LLC Title Page: Shutterstock Images LLC
Contents Page: Shutterstock Images LLC Inside: Netscribes Inc.: 7tl, 7tr, 7bl, 7br, 11t, 11c, 11b, 12, 15tl, 15tr, 15bl, 15br, 19tl, 19tr, 19bl, 19br, 21b, 23t, 23cl, 23cr, 23b, 27tl, 27tr, 27bl, 27br, 31t, 31cl, 31cr, 31bl, 31br, 35tl, 35tr, 35bl, 35br, 39tl, 39tr, 39bl, 39br, 43t, 43cl, 43cr, 43bl, 43br Shutterstock Images LLC: 4, 5t, 5b, 6, 8, 9, 10, 13, 14, 16bl, 16bc, 16br, 17, 18, 20, 21t, 22, 24, 25, 26, 28, 29t, 29b, 30t, 30b, 32, 33t, 33b, 34, 36, 37, 38, 40, 41t, 41b, 42,48

Printed in the United States of America

CPSIA compliance information: Batch #CS12GS: For further information contact Gareth Stevens, New York, New York at 1-800-542-2595.

Contents

Center of the World

Natural barriers surround China's fertile eastern coast. There are high mountains and harsh deserts to the west. To the south and east lie vast oceans. As a result, the ancient Chinese had little contact with people from outside China. For thousands of years, they thought they were the only civilized people on Earth.

The Himalayas in southwestern China are the highest mountains in the world.

Middle Kingdom

In ancient times, most of the people living in China were in the "Middle Kingdom." This area included the coastal plains and river valleys of the central and southern coast. The land had rich soil and plenty of rain. It was perfect for farming. People were also found in the forests on the north coast.

In ancient times, the decorations on a person's clothing indicated his or her position in society.

The Chinese considered the populated coast of China the actual center of Earth.

By the Rivers

China has many rivers that snake east from the mountains. The two largest are the Yangtze and the Huang He, or "Yellow River." These rivers flow through fertile valleys thousands of miles long. When the Chinese first began building settlements, nearly all of them were built on the rivers.

The Chinese were expert shipbuilders. Their sailboats, called junks, could navigate both the rivers and the open sea. Traditional Chinese junks are still in operation.

Close-Up

The rivers carried water that was needed for farming. In addition, they were a source of transportation. The ancient Chinese used the rivers to link inland settlements with the coast. Not everything the rivers brought was good, however. The early Chinese people called their rivers the "Great Sorrow" because annual flooding caused damage.

Find Your Way

The compass originated in China, during the Qin **dynasty**. Ancient sailors used simple compasses to see which way was north. To see how, just follow these directions.

Materials Needed
- Bar magnet
- Needle
- Thread about 6 inches long
- Popsicle stick
- Paper cup
- Glue

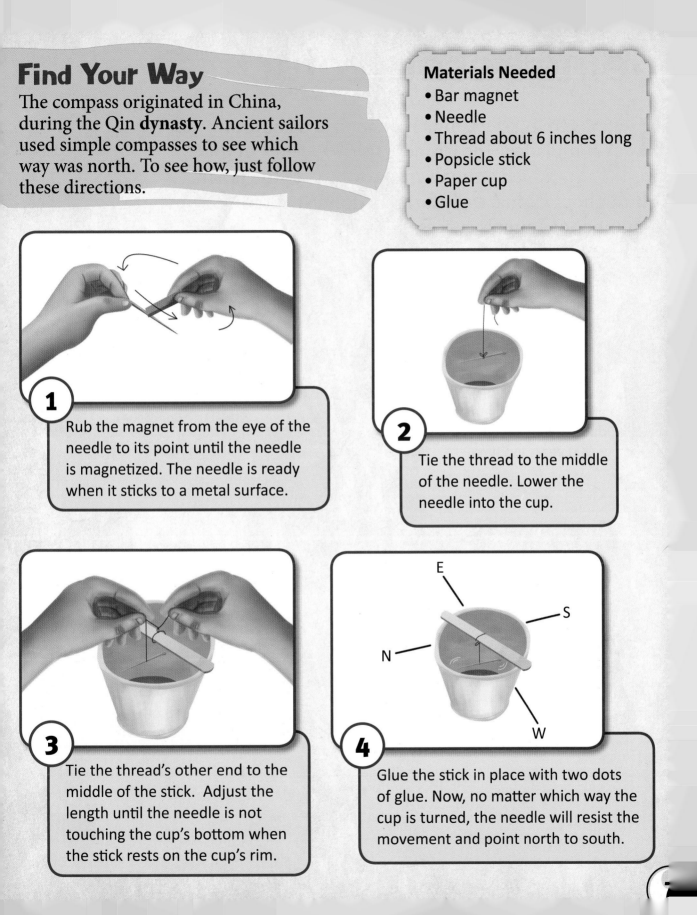

1 Rub the magnet from the eye of the needle to its point until the needle is magnetized. The needle is ready when it sticks to a metal surface.

2 Tie the thread to the middle of the needle. Lower the needle into the cup.

3 Tie the thread's other end to the middle of the stick. Adjust the length until the needle is not touching the cup's bottom when the stick rests on the cup's rim.

4 Glue the stick in place with two dots of glue. Now, no matter which way the cup is turned, the needle will resist the movement and point north to south.

Being Resourceful

Thanks to its size, China had natural resources in abundance. The Chinese mined metals in the west. They hunted animals in the forests of the north. Throughout China, early farmers **domesticated** a number of animals successfully. These creatures included the duck, the pig, and the water buffalo.

Evidence of mining and the use of metals dates back well over 3,000 years in China.

Ahead of Their Time

The ancient Chinese were very inventive. They were the first to make paper and gunpowder. Chinese ironworkers were thousands of years ahead of the metalworkers in Europe. The farmers in China had better plows and higher crop yields than farmers in the West. In many ways, China was the most modern country in the ancient world.

Fireworks were also a Chinese invention.

Turning Up the Heat

One of the reasons the Chinese were so good with metal was their ability to create very hot fires. Early on, the Chinese invented a kind of **bellows** that fed extra air into their fires. These fires were hot enough to **smelt** iron. They were also hot enough to make **porcelain**.

Close-Up

Porcelain is a kind of pottery developed in China. It was fired in a very hot flame and covered with a **glaze**. The result was a shiny, hard material that was easy to clean. It was perfect for storage and cookware. To this day, many people still call fine porcelain dishes "china."

In this particular style of Chinese porcelain, the blue designs are made with cobalt dust and baked right into the white clay.

Play with Clay

The Chinese potters dug their clay from the ground. By digging in your cupboards, you may find the materials you need to make your own clay.

Materials Needed
- Measuring cup
- Salt
- Flour
- Bowl
- Hot water
- Food coloring (optional)
- Container

1 Mix one part salt and two parts flour in the bowl.

2 Add one part hot water and, if desired, food coloring of your choice. Mix thoroughly.

3 Once the material has mixed together enough, you may ply it into whatever shapes you would like. The shapes will air-dry over several days.

4 To keep the clay fresh, store it in a container and refrigerate it. It should keep for about a week.

One Way of Doing Things

Over its long history, different leaders have run China different ways. One of the best-known ways was a system called **Legalism**. Legalism was a way of thinking that was written about by two men named Shang Yang and Han Feizi. They thought that most people were bad, but that rulers could control the bad ways of the people with good laws.

Han Feizi was a member of the Han royal family who studied how princes and kings ruled their people.

Four Kinds of People

Legalists divided people into four classes: the shi, nong, gong, and shang. Shi were scholars and officials. They were considered the most important. Nong were farmers, who formed the second-best class in China. Gong were skilled craftsmen and workers. Shang were the traders. They were the lowest class. People thought of traders as dishonest and greedy.

One of the wonders of the world is the terra-cotta army, an army of clay soldiers and horses at the tomb of Qin Shi Huang, a Chinese emperor who adopted Legalism. Under Legalism, soldiers were not highly respected, but army officers were.

1

Religious Life

Legalism came into acceptance during the period from 475 B.C. to 221 B.C. The Legalists had no class for priests. This is because Legalism did not agree with religion. The Chinese had a number of religions, but under Legalism they were all thought of as false. Being a priest was not thought to be a real job.

Close-Up

The emperor Qin Shi Huang read the work of Han Feizi. At the time, the kingdom of Qin had just beaten the kingdom of Han for control of China. Even though Han Feizi was a member of the rival royal family, Qin Shi Huang sent for him to serve as an adviser. In the end, the emperor did not trust Han Feizi and jailed him. But Qin still adopted Legalism throughout the land.

Qin Shi Huang was a harsh ruler. He feared death, and he sent his officials to search for an **elixir** of life. They never found one.

On Guard

The terra-cotta army, on page 13, guards the tomb of Qin Shi Huang. With the clay you made earlier, you can make your own soldier to protect your nightstand or dresser.

Materials Needed
- Clay
- Toothpick
- Paint and paintbrush

1 Mold the body, head, and legs first. The real terracotta warriors are hollow except for the legs, so they can stand upright. In a smaller size, balance should not be a problem.

2 The statues were dressed as warriors, which generally included a thick robe, boots, and armor. Use some extra clay to give the appearance of clothing.

3 Now, with the toothpick, you can begin to make the smaller details. Carve the face, and make checkers on the body to show your warrior's armor.

4 Let your figure dry and then paint it. Although most of the paint has worn away, Qin Shi Huang's warriors had black hair, pink or white faces, and colorful uniforms.

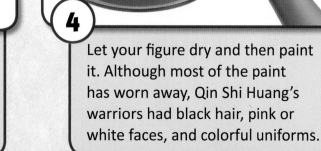

One Land, Many Beliefs

China is the birthplace of a number of world religions. The earliest religions were small and local. They followed gods of nature. Around 600 B.C., a man known as Lao-tzu wrote about the importance of keeping life simple. His belief system came to be known as **Taoism**. Taoists looked for balance between opposite forces called **yin and yang**.

The yin-yang symbol shows balance in nature between opposite energies such as dark and light or female and male. Dragons were yang, and the phoenix, a bird that was reborn from fire, was yin. On Taoist temples, the dragon and phoenix are shown together. In Taoism, nothing is all yin or all yang.

Confucius Says, Mozi Says

Around the same time, two other great thinkers were also attracting followers. Confucius was one of them. He was the thinker behind **Confucianism**. He taught that people would be happiest by accepting their roles in life and doing as they are told. Mozi was the second one. He told his followers, the **Mohists**, to have "universal love" for all others.

Confucius was a well-known schoolteacher whose followers spread his thoughts throughout China.

Ask Grandfather

Though there were a number of big and interesting ideas going around, many people chose to believe in something, and someone, much closer to home. In ancient China, one of the most important beliefs was in **filial piety**. The people prayed to their own dead ancestors. Often they did this by making food offerings.

Close-Up

Filial piety also meant honoring living relatives. Chinese people had to serve and obey their parents. In China, family was sacred. Every good deed that a Chinese person did brought honor to his or her whole family. Every bad deed brought shame.

Filial piety was a core value of both Confucianism and Taoism. When Buddhism spread to China from India, filial piety became part of the Buddhist belief system.

Pet Dragon

The dragon is the most powerful animal in Chinese tradition. At certain points, only the emperor was allowed to wear the dragon symbol. Now, you can have all the power of the dragon. All you need is paper and a few other simple items.

Materials Needed
- Paper
- Pencil
- Colored pencils or markers
- Scissors
- Tape

1 Draw separate outlines of the body and head. Make a long body, about 2 inches wide, that is shaped like a lazy S. Shape the head like a fat numeral 8.

2 Decorate the body and head however you like. Make sure to add the dragon's eyes, snout, and teeth.

3 Cut out the body and head. Take one end of the body and fold back the top half-inch.

4 Fold the body repeatedly every half-inch. Tape the head to one end.

Building Harmony

Chinese buildings are known for their curved roofs and artistic details. Their main goal was to create a sense of **harmony** and order. To do this, many Chinese buildings show **symmetry**. This principle made the buildings look even and balanced. In addition, many Chinese buildings were built in **tiers** to make them strong and stable.

The Forbidden City in Beijing contains religious and government buildings built in the classic Chinese style. To see an example of symmetry, think of an imaginary line down the middle of this building. One side reflects the other.

The Great Wall

For hundreds of years, China was under constant attack from people known as the Huns. The Huns came from Mongolia in the north. They never conquered much land, but they **pillaged** Chinese villages and farms. To keep the Huns away, the Chinese princes began building walls. Over the next 2,000 years, these walls grew together to form the Great Wall of China.

The Great Wall is 5,500 miles long and has guardhouses and castles built in at intervals along its length. Today some sections have become tourist attractions.

The Great Wall of China

The Qin first connected the sections of the Great Wall around 200 B.C. Today the structure is visible from space.

In the House

The size and shape of Chinese homes varied based on where they were and who owned them. Typical Chinese building materials were stone, wood, and mud brick. A common farmhouse had a few rooms, a garden, and sometimes a family **shrine**. Wealthier people had larger, sturdier homes. Many were made in the same style as government buildings.

In parts of China, houses were always built with their doors facing south to keep out the cold north wind.

Close-Up

Unlike their neighbors in Japan, the Chinese filled their homes with furniture and decorations. In a middle-class home, a visitor would find tables, chairs, and storage. Beams and wall sections were painted or carved. There were often scrolls with paintings or **calligraphy** hanging on the walls.

Light the Way

Chinese paper lanterns are a sign of celebration. The ancient Chinese also placed them around their homes for good luck. Now, you can make your own luck with this homemade paper lantern.

1 Using the ruler, draw a straight line along the shorter edge of the paper, about half an inch from the edge. Cut and set this strip aside; it will be used as the handle.

2 Fold the paper in half lengthwise. Starting at the crease, make about seven cuts, equally spaced and equally long. Leave at least 2 inches of space between the cut and the edge of the paper.

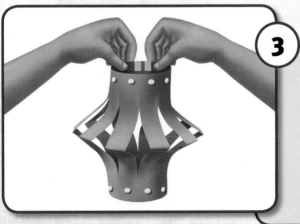

3 Unfold the paper. If you want to decorate your lantern, use the side with the fold sticking out. When done, bring the ends together and tape them firmly. Now staple both ends of the paper strip to one of the open ends of the lantern.

Early Experts

Chinese people were some of the first in the world to grow their own food. Scientists have found evidence of farming from over 10,000 years ago. Most of the early farms were in the river valleys. This was because the soil in the valleys was rich and did not need plowing.

Due to flooding, farmers who lived along the rivers often had to rebuild their houses.

Rice grows fast, but it takes a lot of work to harvest.

Crops to Spare

The first crops in China were grains such as **millet**. A bit later, the Chinese learned to grow rice, which grows fast and takes up less land. Using bronze and iron, the Chinese made tools like the plow. With better tools, they were able to dig canals to move water. This greatly increased the amount of farmland that could be used.

The Real Chinese Food

The food that ancient Chinese people ate was very different from what is found at today's Chinese take-out restaurant. The ancient Chinese ate vegetables and game meat such as deer. They also ate all kinds of seafood. Later on, Buddhism spread to China. Buddhists did not eat meat, so the Chinese invented a bean curd called **tofu** for protein.

Tea grows in the wild in China. Chinese people have been drinking tea for thousands of years.

Close-Up

For the Chinese, farming and cooking were one process. The best farmers and cooks worked together to feed the emperors. They created an entire style of cooking, called **imperial cuisine**. Its dishes were only for royalty. Cooks for the emperor got a lot of respect. Some of them even became political figures.

Go Fish

In Cantonese, a Chinese language, the word for "fish" is also the word for "surplus." That's because people in southern China caught a lot of fish! Now, here is a way to make fish with surplus art supplies.

Materials Needed
- Paper plate
- Scissors
- Glue
- Wrapping or tissue paper
- Googly eye from craft store or a button

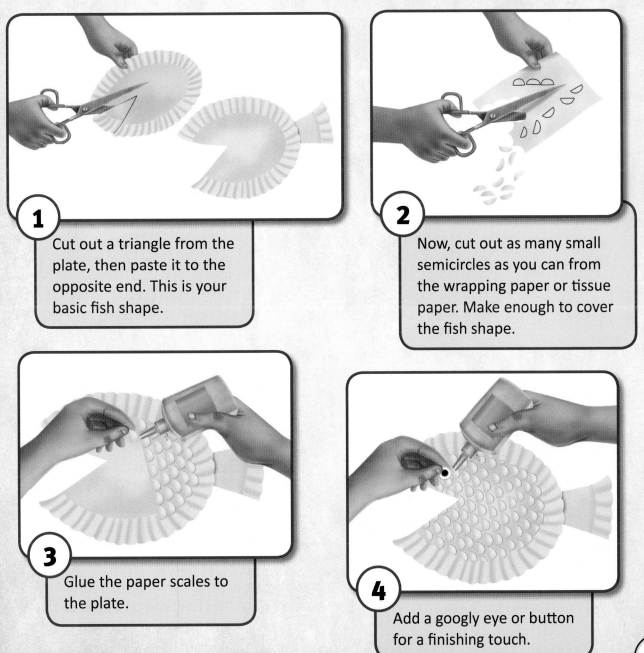

1 Cut out a triangle from the plate, then paste it to the opposite end. This is your basic fish shape.

2 Now, cut out as many small semicircles as you can from the wrapping paper or tissue paper. Make enough to cover the fish shape.

3 Glue the paper scales to the plate.

4 Add a googly eye or button for a finishing touch.

Dressing Lightly

Over thousands of years and many different dynasties, Chinese clothing changed a great deal. Early on, men and women wore basic **tunics** and trousers or skirts. Later on, they switched to robes and dresses. Buddhists had their own style of simple clothing. All the eras and groups used **silk** to make light, comfortable clothing.

The **douli** is a traditional, cone-shaped hat that blocks the sun and keeps the wearer cool. The hats can be made of fabric, straw, or bamboo.

In the Dark

The Chinese had distinct beliefs about color in their clothing. Chinese tastes ran toward dark, rich colors. This is because the dark fabrics were harder to produce and more expensive. Wearing dark or very bright colors in daily life was a sign of wealth. Middle-class people had dark clothes for special occasions.

Dragon robes were made of the finest silk and were covered with detailed embroidery.

Today's monks dress in much the same way as they did in ancient times.

Rings and Things

Earrings were very popular in ancient China. Both women and men wore them. Most jewelry made at the time was silver or copper. But the jewelers also made **cloisonné** items. Cloisonné is a way of decorating metal items. Basically, the Chinese melted glass on a metal base. They used glass of many colors and linked shapes to make patterns. Their jewelry often showed animals.

Close-Up

Chinese women carried handheld fans. Their fans were made from bamboo and paper. They were designed to fold up for storage. Many of the fans were decorated with artwork and writing. In China's hot southern region, the fans were especially handy. Even in cooler areas, women still carried them for decoration.

The ancient Chinese had many names for fans. The terms used ranged in meaning from "cool friends" to "hiding face."

Working the Fields

Chinese peasants often wore doulis to shade their heads and necks from the hot sun. You can make your own douli out of poster board.

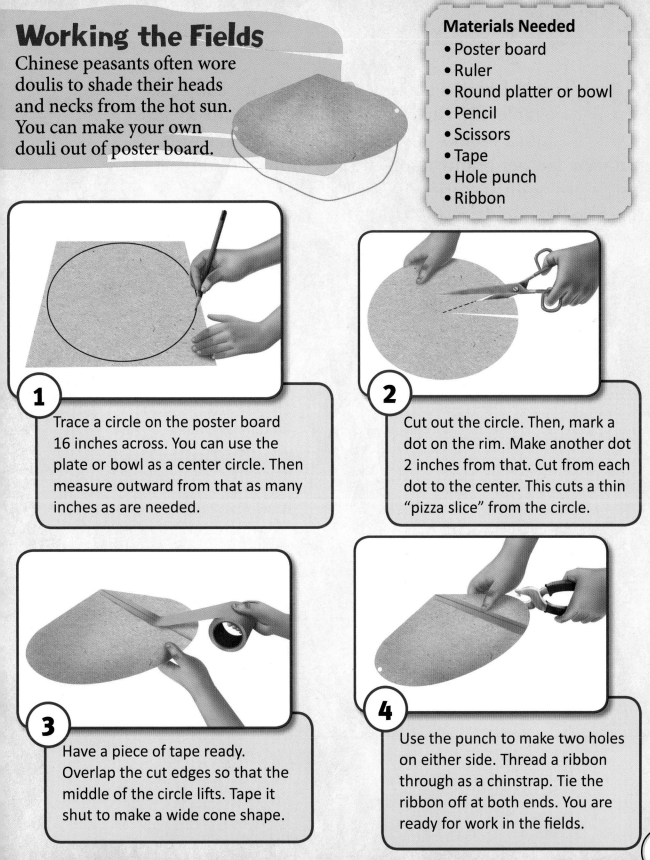

1 Trace a circle on the poster board 16 inches across. You can use the plate or bowl as a center circle. Then measure outward from that as many inches as are needed.

2 Cut out the circle. Then, mark a dot on the rim. Make another dot 2 inches from that. Cut from each dot to the center. This cuts a thin "pizza slice" from the circle.

3 Have a piece of tape ready. Overlap the cut edges so that the middle of the circle lifts. Tape it shut to make a wide cone shape.

4 Use the punch to make two holes on either side. Thread a ribbon through as a chinstrap. Tie the ribbon off at both ends. You are ready for work in the fields.

A Higher Art

Many Chinese artists chose to draw religious subjects. For example, the yin-yang symbol showed up on Taoist art. The Buddhist monks in southern and western China produced another brand of art. It often showed Buddha and illustrated Buddhist stories. Followers of Confucius and Mozi also liked to draw and paint their leaders.

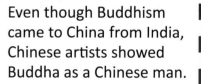

Even though Buddhism came to China from India, Chinese artists showed Buddha as a Chinese man.

Carving a Reputation

Carving was a popular Chinese art form. Carvings were made from wood, ivory, and stones such as **jade**. Chinese carvers tried to use the natural shapes and swirls in their materials to guide their carving. The results were very detailed. Many carvings were animal shapes. Others looked like people and things in nature.

Chinese prized jade above all other stones. They considered it the "stone of heaven."

Painting a Picture

The Chinese used the same tools and inks for painting as they did for calligraphy. Because of this, many **scribes** also painted. This is why Chinese paintings often have writing and poetry mixed with pictures. The words are meant to work with the pictures, so they were much like serious comic books.

Xieyi paintings often show exaggerated versions of landscapes.

Close-Up

A very famous Chinese style of painting is **xieyi**. Xieyi paintings show nature in an exaggerated style. Many xieyi paintings are black and white. They usually have some kind of poetry or saying, which is sometimes written in red to stand out.

Blossoms in Winter

In Chinese culture, plum blossoms are highly respected for their ability to withstand winter. You can make your own Chinese blossom art, with a personal twist.

Materials Needed
- Heavy paper
- Brown paint and paintbrush
- Pink tissue paper
- Glue
- Green and blue tissue paper (optional)

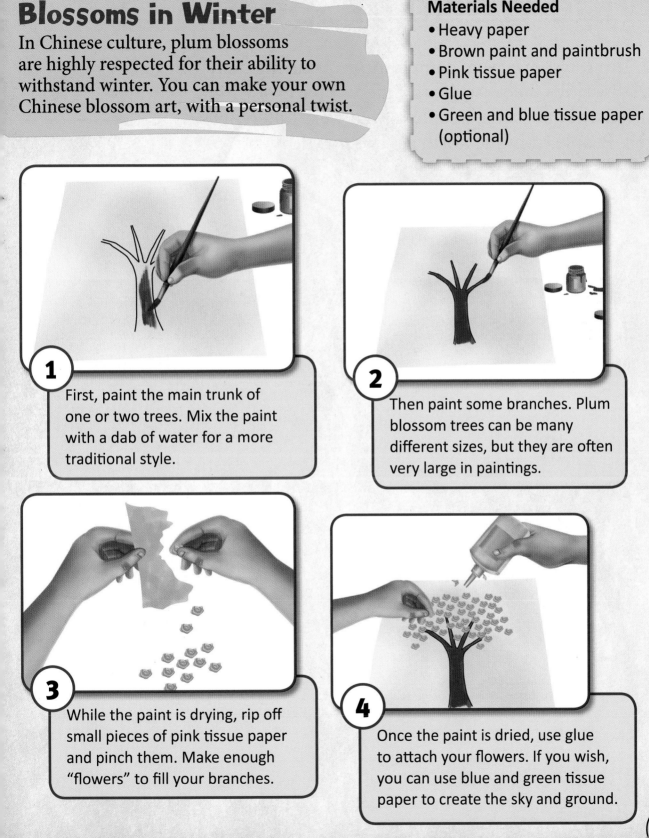

1 First, paint the main trunk of one or two trees. Mix the paint with a dab of water for a more traditional style.

2 Then paint some branches. Plum blossom trees can be many different sizes, but they are often very large in paintings.

3 While the paint is drying, rip off small pieces of pink tissue paper and pinch them. Make enough "flowers" to fill your branches.

4 Once the paint is dried, use glue to attach your flowers. If you wish, you can use blue and green tissue paper to create the sky and ground.

Wide World of Sports

Chinese sports were competitions featuring daily life skills. Because life in different parts of China varied, the sports the people played were different as well. People from the north and west rode horses in daily life. For sport, they raced horses and competed to show other riding skills. People on the coasts and rivers had swimming and boat races.

Everybody Was . . .

When the Qin first conquered China, they banned all weapons. Without weapons, people needed methods of fighting with their hands and feet. They came up with martial arts such as **kung fu**. Early kung fu was deadly. However, when weapons were allowed again, kung fu and its cousins became sports.

Dragon boat races are traditional rowing competitions from the Yangtze River region that are still held throughout the world today.

Kung fu is just one of many schools of ancient Chinese martial arts. Many groups, from the imperial army to Buddhist monks, developed their own styles of fighting.

It was a widely believed myth that mahjong was created by Confucius himself.

Peaceful Games

Not all Chinese games were physical or violent. Puzzles were a favorite pastime for the ancient Chinese. A **tangram** set came with five triangles, one square, and one parallelogram. These could be arranged to make all sorts of new shapes. Ancient tangram sets were made of ivory, soft stone, or metal.

Close-Up

The Chinese also invented domino tiles, which they used to play competitive puzzle games. **Mahjong** was another tile game. Mahjong tiles were made of ivory or mother-of-pearl. They each had numbers or pictures related to Confucianism.

Shaping Up

Tangram sets were sometimes called the "seven pieces of cleverness." You can make your own set to see why this is so.

Materials Needed
- Poster board
- Ruler
- Pencil
- Scissors

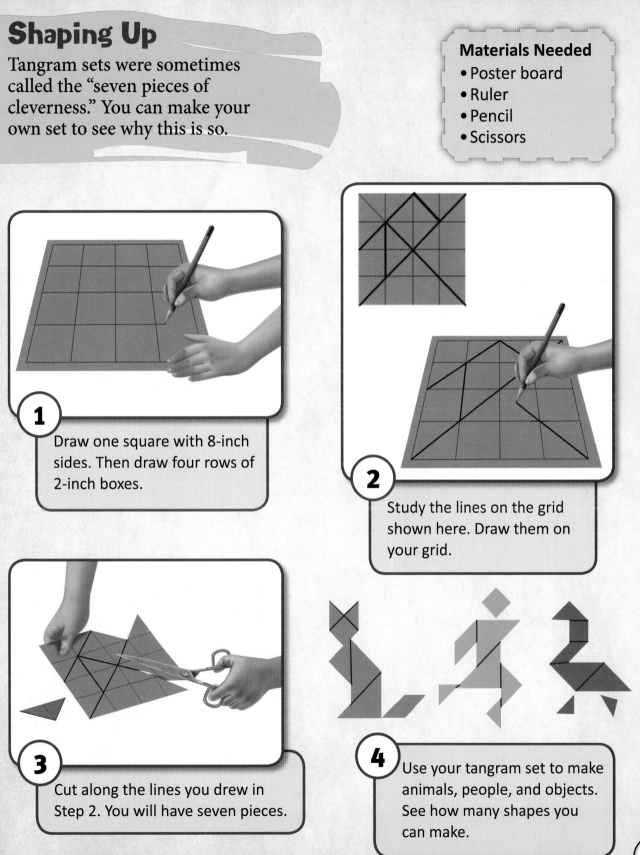

1 Draw one square with 8-inch sides. Then draw four rows of 2-inch boxes.

2 Study the lines on the grid shown here. Draw them on your grid.

3 Cut along the lines you drew in Step 2. You will have seven pieces.

4 Use your tangram set to make animals, people, and objects. See how many shapes you can make.

School Is Everything

There was a saying in ancient China that "if no education is given to a child, his nature will go bad." China had a big private school system. Religious groups, nobles, and the government all set up schools. Confucius and Mozi were both teachers. Any family that could afford it sent their children to some kind of school.

At school, children learned poetry and philosophy as well as reading and writing.

Passing the Test

A key part of Chinese education was testing. The **Keju** was the exam that was developed in late imperial China. It had two parts. The first was an arts test that included writing, painting, law, and other disciplines. The second was a martial arts display. Students who did well were placed in government jobs or the military based on the skills they showed during the test.

The Keju system was put in place around A.D. 600 and lasted until 1908.

Writing with Style

Even in ancient times, the Chinese alphabet had hundreds of letters. Learning to write took a lot of time. Students were expected to write perfectly. They spent hours scratching out lines in sand to practice penmanship. Paper and ink were expensive, so they wanted to be sure they had mastered the strokes before actually writing.

Place Yourself in China

Would you enjoy calligraphy?

Calligraphy was said to use the "four treasures of the study." These were the pen, the paper, the ink stick, and the ink slab.

Close-Up

The most delicate form of Chinese writing was calligraphy. Masters of calligraphy used large brushes and black ink to write. Brushstrokes had to be fluid and fast. An interrupted brushstroke would leave a puddle of ink and ruin the whole paper.

Eight Principles of Yong

Here, you will be practicing the Chinese symbol *yong*, which means "eternity." This is a common beginner's task because the symbol for *yong* requires the eight most basic brushstrokes.

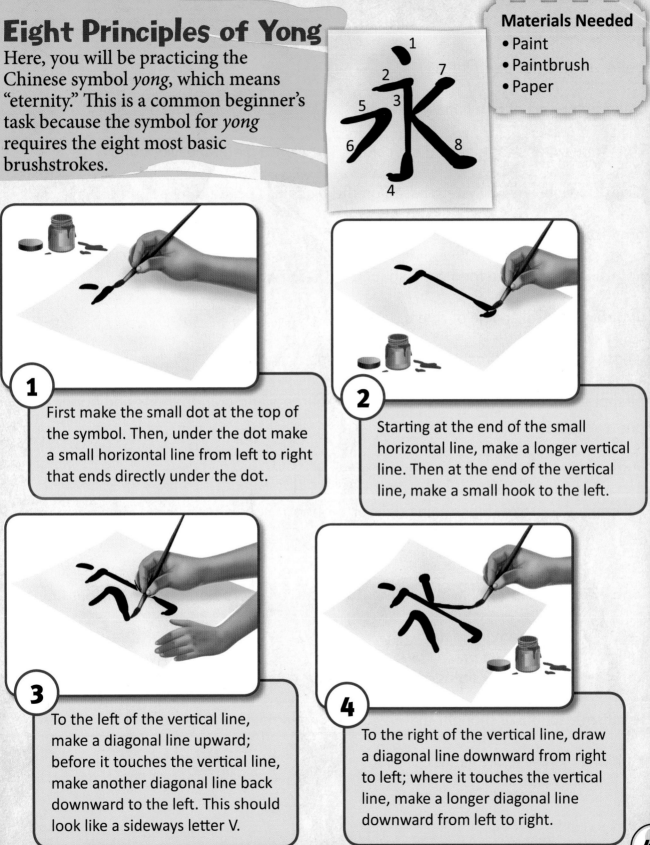

Materials Needed
- Paint
- Paintbrush
- Paper

1

First make the small dot at the top of the symbol. Then, under the dot make a small horizontal line from left to right that ends directly under the dot.

2

Starting at the end of the small horizontal line, make a longer vertical line. Then at the end of the vertical line, make a small hook to the left.

3

To the left of the vertical line, make a diagonal line upward; before it touches the vertical line, make another diagonal line back downward to the left. This should look like a sideways letter V.

4

To the right of the vertical line, draw a diagonal line downward from right to left; where it touches the vertical line, make a longer diagonal line downward from left to right.

Glossary

bellows—tool for pumping air

calligraphy—art of fine handwriting

cloisonné—craft made by melting colored glass onto a metal background

Confucianism—belief system based on the teachings of the thinker Confucius

domesticated—taught to live in captivity

douli—Chinese name for a cone-shaped hat worn by field-workers

dynasty—unbroken line of rulers

elixir—a substance capable of prolonging life

filial piety—obedience and service to one's parents and grandparents and honor to one's ancestors

glaze—clear, shiny hard covering on porcelain

harmony—sense of things being right or proper or in balance

imperial cuisine—style of cooking done only for the emperor

jade—green stone with swirl markings that was considered precious in ancient China

Keju—imperial exam in China

kung fu—one of many styles of Chinese martial arts

Legalism—school of thought that says rulers need harsh laws to control the people

mahjong—Chinese tile game

millet—grain that can be ground or cooked in stew

Mohists—people who follow Mozi's teachings of "universal love"

pillaged—robbed and destroyed

porcelain—hard material made by firing special clay at high temperatures

scribe—someone who copies manuscripts

shrine—decorated place for prayer or reflection

silk—cloth made from silkworm fibers that is very light and comfortable

smelt—to melt material for the purpose of separating the pure metals

symmetry—similarity seen on two sides of a dividing line

tangram—puzzle set that offers a set of simple shapes to make pictures

Taoism—belief in living a life balanced between opposing forces in nature

tiers—easy-to-see levels of land or of a structure, which look like steps

tofu—bean curd, which has high protein and can be used as a meat substitute

tunics—T-shirt-shaped clothing that falls to the knee or ankle

xieyi—style of painting that shows exaggerated scenes of nature, often in black-and-white

yin and yang—in Taoism, the two opposite forces that make up the universe

For Further Information

Books

Ancient China. Arthur Cotterell. (DK Eyewitness, 2005)

The Ancient Chinese. Virginia Schomp. (Children's Press, 2005)

The Emperor's Silent Army: Terracotta Warriors of Ancient China. Jane O'Connor. (Viking, 2002)

McGraw-Hill's Chinese Illustrated Dictionary. Editors. (McGraw-Hill, 2009)

Web Sites

Ancient China for Kids
http://china.mrdonn.org/

What's the story behind chopsticks? What happens at the Chinese Lantern Festival? This student-friendly site covers interesting subjects, including old Chinese proverbs.

Kidipede: Ancient China
http://www.historyforkids.org/learn/china/

To find out more about Chinese inventions, such as gunpowder, and to look deeper into daily life in ancient times, explore the catalog of information on the Kidipede site.

KidsKonnect.com: Ancient China
http://www.kidskonnect.com/subject-index/16-history/252-ancient-china.html

This Internet gateway starts with fast facts about the ancient Chinese and links to information about Chinese dynasties, the Great Wall, maps, and more.

Social Studies for Kids: Ancient China
http://www.socialstudiesforkids.com/subjects/ancientchina.htm

Learn where the Silk Road started, read more about early Eastern beliefs, and look into other fascinating aspects of ancient China.

Publisher's note to educators and parents: Our editors have carefully reviewed these websites to ensure that they are suitable for students. Many websites change frequently, however, and we cannot guarantee that a site's future contents will continue to meet our high standards of quality and educational value. Be advised that students should be closely supervised whenever they access the Internet.

Index

Things to Think About and Do

Final Word

Chinese fables were little stories about people or animals doing silly things. The fables always had a lesson at the end.

One example is the story of "His Spear Against His Shield":

A man of the state of Chu had a spear and a shield for sale.
He was loud in praises of his shield. "My shield is so strong that nothing can pierce it through."
He also sang praises of his spear. "My spear is so strong that it can pierce through anything."
"What would happen," he was asked, "if your spear is used to pierce your shield?"
It is impossible for an impenetrable shield to coexist with a spear that finds nothing impenetrable.

Try It!

Think of a good lesson that you have learned the hard way. Now try to write the story of how you learned it. Keep it as short as you can, and then state the lesson at the end.